Original title:
The Lyrical Logs of Lore

Copyright © 2025 Creative Arts Management OÜ
All rights reserved.

Author: Elias Montgomery
ISBN HARDBACK: 978-1-80567-370-5
ISBN PAPERBACK: 978-1-80567-669-0

Tales From the Twilight Tides

A crab in a hat danced on the shore,
His friends all chuckled, then begged for more.
With a flippery flip and a jiggly jig,
He made the seaweed sway, oh so big.

The seagulls squabbled over discarded fries,
As the fish told jokes in their watery guise.
One fish said, "Why did the shark cross the bay?"
"To get to the other tide, or so they say!"

An octopus laughed, with ink on the side,
He scribbled a poem, oh how he tried!
But every time he reached for the pen,
He squirted out ink, and scribbled again.

The starfish debated the best dance moves,
While the barnacles grumbled, tired of grooves.
They formed a conga line, slow and quite steady,
With each wobble and wiggle, the sea felt ready.

So when you stroll by the twinkling foam,
Remember the creatures who call it home.
They dance and they play under moon's soft glow,
In their comical lives, they steal the show!

Whispers in the Canopy

Up in the trees where squirrels flirt,
A wise old owl wears a tiny shirt.
Laughter echoes from branch to branch,
While raccoons don hats for a silly dance.

The birds chirp secrets, oh what a show,
A squirrel slipped, landed in a dough.
From leafy crowns to roots below,
Nature's jesters put on a glow.

Echoes of Enchanted Timber

A lumberjack talks to a rocking chair,
It tells him secrets, but he doesn't care.
Logs laugh aloud, they do a jig,
As fairies drop nuts—oh, what a big twig!

Mossy stones play hide-and-seek,
While chipmunks plan a paintball streak.
The trees wear socks, quite colorful,
A forest party, wonderful and full.

Chronicles of the Forest Heart

A bear in a tutu, what a sight!
Dancing with owls, oh what delight.
They spin and twirl, making quite a mess,
With berries flying, in a fruity dress.

The pinecones gossip, they've got the scoop,
While frogs form a most eccentric troupe.
A hedgehog juggles with sticks and leaves,
Laughing so hard, the ground still heaves.

Serenades of the Sylvan Path

A fox in a bowtie makes a fine toast,
To ants marching fast, it's a most merry host.
Beneath the moon, all creatures prance,
In this merry wood, everyone has a chance.

The night sky twinkles, stars play along,
Singing sweet tunes to nature's throng.
With giggles and chuckles filling the air,
Every critter joins in for a wild affair.

Lyricism in the Luminous Night

Under the moon's bright, silly grin,
Cats play chess; who will win?
Stars twinkle like winking lights,
Dancing critters hold late-night fights.

Fireflies hum their glowing tunes,
Squirrels juggle acorns, watch those balloons!
Laughter echoes through the trees,
As owls hoot jokes, bringing us to our knees.

Chronicles Beyond the Horizon

Baboons debate in bowler hats,
While penguins plot to steal the bats.
Cacti wear sunglasses, looking so cool,
While llamas line dance, breaking the rule.

Over the hills where giggles reside,
Unicorns brag, with a sparkly stride.
Each sunset paints a comical scene,
Life's a joke, not quite routine.

Twilight's Telling Tradition

As nightfall creeps, shadows begin,
Ducks in pajamas swirl with a spin.
Turtles race to the finish line,
While rabbits sip tea, feeling so fine.

Balloons float high, waving their tails,
A snail tells stories of grand old trails.
Laughter in the air, a delightful scent,
In this whimsical world, we are all well spent.

Parables of the Wandering Spirit

A ghost with a grin, a quirky delight,
Spins silly tales in the moon's soft light.
He trips on his chains, oh what a sight,
As goblins join in, tongues wagging in fright.

Dancing with shadows, they waltz down the lane,
Each step is a giggle, a tickle, a strain.
Fortunes foretold with a wink and a cheer,
In this playful dance, there's nothing to fear.

Ballads of the Hidden Grove

In the grove where squirrels dance,
A rabbit took a silly stance.
He wore a hat, quite upside down,
And made the flowers laugh and frown.

The trees all giggled with delight,
As frogs joined in with leaps so bright.
A snail recited jokes so slow,
While crickets played a lively show.

Legends Carved in Stone

On a boulder big, a wise old crow,
Claimed he knew how to put on a show.
He juggled acorns, two in each wing,
And sang a tune that made the rocks sing.

Nearby, a tortoise with dreams to soar,
Wore a cape made of leaves from yore.
He practiced flying, but fell with a thud,
Landing squarely in a puddle of mud.

Melodies of the Misty Vale

In the vale where shadows play tag,
A fox wore socks that made a wag.
He pranced about with a cheeky grin,
Declaring he'd dance till the sun wore thin.

A bear with a penchant for rhymes,
Chanted verses in odd, funny times.
The owls rolled their eyes in disdain,
As the wind joined in with a silly refrain.

Tapestry of Echoes

In a meadow where echoes do play,
Lived a goat that loved to sway.
With each bleat, the hills would giggle,
As he danced about with a funny wiggle.

A horse with a laugh so bright,
Told tales of his epic fight.
Against a wall of hay so strong,
That took a nap and snored along.

Fragments of Forgotten Time

In the attic, dust bunnies play,
Juggling old hats, in a silly way.
Grandpa's socks dance on the floor,
While history giggles at the door.

A clock ticks back, then leaps ahead,
Whispering secrets no one has read.
A cat with glasses reads a book,
And laughs at the world with a quirky look.

A photo frame winks, full of cheer,
It captured a moment that was once dear.
Invisible ink spills tales of glee,
Of pickle fights and climbing a tree.

A squeaky chair begins to hum,
Reciting tales of where we're from.
In this nook where laughter climbs,
We're lost in fragments of funny times.

Rhymes of the Realm Beyond

In a land where shoes all squeak with glee,
A cow wears a tie, sipping sweet tea.
The sun cracks jokes with the cheeky moon,
While stars dance wildly, humming a tune.

Goblin chefs bake pies that fly,
With each tasty nibble, you'll want to cry.
Wizards barter with spinning plates,
Casting spells while discussing dates.

A dragon throws a surprise parade,
With candy canes and a wobbly charade.
Knights in pajamas clash with soft pillows,
As unicorns giggle atop their rainbows.

Rhymes flutter lightly in the breeze,
Telling tales that tickle with ease.
In this realm where laughter's profound,
Joy is found in each silly sound.

Prose of the Dreaming Drifters

Dreamers wander with a grin so wide,
Chasing rainbows on a silly slide.
Mice in costumes engage in a play,
As elephants dance in a curious way.

Jelly beans rain from fluffy clouds,
While popcorn falls, attracting crowds.
The sky's a canvas of giggling hues,
Where laughter paints the evening news.

Kites shaped like fish swim through the air,
Tickling the clouds without a care.
A mermaid sings to a soap bubble choir,
While most of the world just wants to retire.

In prose where fantasies interlace,
Funny moments find their place.
Drifting dreams with smiles that gleam,
Life's a whimsical, funny theme.

Echoes Through Evergreen

In a forest where the squirrels wear ties,
And trees whisper secrets with glamorous sighs.
Bears solve riddles on a picnic blanket,
While porcupines tease and the owls crank it.

Bamboo dances, sways to the beat,
As raccoons tap dance with nimble feet.
The flowers join in with laughter loud,
Creating a symphony that draws a crowd.

Echoes bounce from trunk to trunk,
Tickling creatures in a merry funk.
Each leaf tells tales from ages past,
Of funny happenings that forever last.

Through evergreens, the giggles flow,
As nature paints a comedic show.
In every shadow and light that beams,
The echoes carry our silliest dreams.

Harmonics of Heartfelt Histories

In days of yore, a cat wore shoes,
Dancing to tunes no one could choose.
A dragon served tea with a pompous air,
While knights played chess in their colorful wear.

A bard sang songs of odd balloon fights,
Where unicorns pranced under disco lights.
They laughed and joked, oh what a sight,
As fairies cheered from their perch in flight.

Brave squirrels battled in marshmallow wars,
While wise old owls traded candy scores.
Every tale hashed out a giggly twist,
In jokes and puns that none could resist.

Refrains of the Recovered Realm

In a realm forgotten, there stood a tree,
Where gummy bears danced and sang with glee.
A wizard at dawn brewed cola with flair,
And knights traded tales of their odd pet bear.

A jester cracked jokes, oh what a delight,
As trolls played hopscotch from morning to night.
With pies in their faces and laughter so loud,
They formed a strange, giggling, joyful crowd.

The elves held a feast of spaghetti and cheese,
While goblins broke records for hiccuping bees.
Each story was spun with mischief and cheer,
In the odd little world where nonsense held dear.

Ancient Melodies in Moonlight

By the silver moon sat a sleepy goat,
Singing to stars while bobbing his coat.
A chorus of frogs took the stage nearby,
While foxes crooned songs in a musical spy.

An owl hooted beats with a tap of his wing,
As raccoons joined in for a late-night fling.
A grumpy old troll played maracas with sass,
While hedgehogs rolled by in a disco-class.

With each little note, the night came alive,
In unexpected ways that made laughter thrive.
And tales of the oddest of things would unfold,
In rhythms so silly, legends turned gold.

Dreams of the Daydreaming Dawn

When dawn broke through with a giggly yawn,
The rooster wore shades and danced on the lawn.
While pancakes flew high from the skillet's base,
An army of toast rallied up for the race.

The sunny side eggs formed a bold brigade,
As syrupy rivers through waffles cascaded.
They twirled and they whirled in a breakfast parade,
Creating grand tales that'll never fade.

With jelly bean soldiers and a donut king,
They brought joy to mornings, a glorious fling.
In dreams of delight, all creatures conspired,
For laughter and fun were truly inspired.

Proverbs of the Patient Trees

When winds whisper secrets low,
Old oak chuckles, sways just so.
Birch giggles, drops her leaves with flair,
"Patience, friends, is half the prayer."

Spruce stands proud, a wise old sage,
Says, "Don't let life turn you to rage.
Grow slow, take your time, that's the key,
Or you might end up like a tumbleweed!"

The willow's bends, a humorous sight,
"Flexibility's the answer, alright!
When life pushes you to the brink,
Just sway with the breeze—don't overthink."

Maples laugh, dressed in golden hues,
"Celebrate mistakes, they're just like blues.
Fall down, get up; repeat with cheer,
For laughter's the syrup we all hold dear!"

Dreams in the Dappled Shade

Beneath the branches, shadows play,
Squirrels dream in a breezy ballet.
With each twist and twirl, they make a scene,
Chasing lost nuts, oh what a routine!

A sleepy fox, he ponders wide,
"Do dreams count if I nap outside?"
As dappled light filters through the leaves,
He dreams of cheese, and whirls, and thieves!

The sunbeams giggle, as they peek through,
Tickling the fawns, all covered in dew.
"Catch us if you can," they gleefully shout,
But the deer are too sly, full of doubt.

In cozy nooks of playful shade,
A turtle's slow wins the parade.
"When life's a race, go at your pace,
Surprise them all with a steady grace!"

Stories in the Leaves' Dance

As leaves unfurl, the stories sprout,
Tales of mischief, giggles about.
A crow caws tales of the morning's mess,
With crumbs left on the squirrel's dress!

"Did you hear how the wind got bold?
Swirled the leaves; what a sight to behold!
They twirled like dancers, with flair and spin,
Until one poor branch broke with a grin!"

Dancing shadows weave fables here,
Of acorns that roll with nothing to fear.
And as the moon glows, adding light,
The whispers of night take playful flight.

Each fluttering leaf, a giggle it shares,
Of elks in sneakers, and owls in chairs.
Nature's comedy, lively and bright,
In the forest's heart, laughter takes flight!

Echoes of the Elderwood

In the elder's arms, secrets reside,
With tales of moonlit bears, so wide.
"Did you see the raccoon's silly prance?
He danced on the log, hoping for a chance!"

Echoes of laughter ripple through time,
As critters recount their tales in rhyme.
"The owl hooted loud when the cat fell down,
Chasing his tail, he wore a frown!"

The breeze brings whispers of olden days,
Of happy mischief in funny ways.
Every rustle calls forth echoes of glee,
As history tickles the tips of each tree.

So gather around, where stories entwine,
In the dance of the branches, all will align.
For in the elder's embrace, you will see,
A legacy woven with joy—oh, so free!

Visions of the Forest Veins

In the heart of the woods, funny critters dance,
Squirrels in tuxedos, a nutty romance.
Trees gossip merrily, whispering tales,
While mushrooms giggle in their tiny trails.

Bears breakdancing on roots, oh what a sight,
Raccoons playing poker far into the night.
An owl with glasses reads stories aloud,
Cheering the forest, it's all quite a crowd!

Frogs jump in concert, a slippery choir,
While fireflies flash like stars of a choir.
Branches shake hands with the passing breeze,
Nature's own comedy, sure to please!

Come join the fun on this whimsical spree,
Beckoned by laughter beneath the tall trees.
Laughter echoes and the night won't cease,
In this silly paradise, joy is our lease.

Diary of the Wandering Branch

Oh, the tales the branches could write in their book,
A wooden detective, like a sly little rook.
They'd tell of their travels, how far they had roamed,
From mountaintops lush to the den where they loomed.

A branch once fell in love with a rock,
But their romance ended in a terrible shock.
The rock was too heavy, the branch feeling weak,
Crushed by rejection, it started to squeak.

Once it tried to climb but got stuck in a thorn,
In a patch of wild roses, feeling forlorn.
With giggles of ants and the squirrels' loud cheer,
It vowed to keep wandering, no hint of fear.

Each twist and each turn holds a whimsical clue,
In forests of wonder, adventures brand new.
The journey of branches, a diary so grand,
Filled with goofy moments across this vast land.

Carols of the Crescent Grove

In the crescent grove, the shadows do sway,
As trees break into carols, come join their ballet.
Twigs tap dance quietly, leaves rustle with glee,
While hedgehogs harmonize in perfect esprit.

A chorus of crickets join in the fun,
Warming the night with the songs they have spun.
Rabbits acrobats leap for joy and surprise,
They stretch in the moonlight, under bright skies.

The snails form a band with a drum made of stone,
While beetles on banjos parade all alone.
A merry procession of critters so spry,
In crescent grove's concert, the laughter will fly.

As the stars twinkle bright, the shadows will wane,
Nature sings of its joy, never a frown or disdain.
With fun like wildflowers that bloom and then sway,
In the grove, all are welcome, hip-hip-hooray!

Layers of Love in the Leaf Fall

As autumn leaves tumble and swirl all around,
The trees share their secrets, the whispers resound.
A leaf fell in love with a big cozy mound,
And here in its warmth, new friendships are found.

The acorns made jokes, they rolled on the ground,
As squirrels did gymnastics, their talents renowned.
The branches applaud, as a leaf takes a dive,
Creating a spectacle, truly alive!

Caterpillars chuckle at blossoms in bloom,
While mushrooms erupt with a pop and a zoom.
They dance in the sunlight, a colorful ball,
In layers of laughter, this joy they recall.

Though seasons may change and the cold winds may call,
The warmth of their fun builds a love that won't fall.
So gather the laughter, the giggles, the cheer,
In nature's grand party, love's always near!

Elysian Echoes of Existence

In a land where squirrels wear hats,
And butterflies dance with the chitchat.
Caterpillars twist on the floor,
While daisies giggle and ask for more.

Clouds have tea with the moonlight,
While frogs eat cake, what a sight!
The trees tell jokes to passing bees,
As they sting the flowers with tales of tease.

A turtle raced a speedy hare,
In roller skates, what a rare affair!
Libelous whispers of foxes in jest,
Found their own egg, oh what a quest!

So join the laughter and the cheer,
In this land, there's never a fear.
For every giggle and every cheer,
Makes life a circus year after year.

Verses From the Vortex

In a whirlpool of endless pranks,
Fish wear sunglasses, gather in ranks.
Octopuses juggle with grace and flair,
While seaweed tango without a care.

The sun throws pies at the cheeky moon,
While stars hum a catchy tune.
Comets dressed in pastel gowns,
Sashay past planets while no one frowns.

Ants hold a feast in the grass so green,
Sipping on nectar, a fancy scene.
Ladybugs gossip through the night,
Over distant tales of flight.

So spin in the vortex, dance and prance,
With silly creatures in a merry trance.
The universe winks with vibrant delight,
As dreams turn to laughter, shining bright.

Poems of the Primordial Past

Dinosaurs battled in bowler hats,
Playing poker with raccoons and bats.
The Earth was a stage for all to see,
With laughter echoing through every tree.

Cavemen painted their toes with glee,
Doodling on walls, as wild as can be.
While mammoths played hide and seek,
In woolly coats, unique and chic.

Volcanoes erupted with confetti and noise,
As fireflies danced, oh what joys!
In this prehistoric festivity,
The past was alive with creativity.

So remember those days, both funny and wild,
Where laughter ruled, every adult and child.
In the annals of time, let giggles last,
In poems rich with humor from the past.

Timeless Whimsies of Nature

In gardens where whispers paint the air,
Rose bushes flaunt their knickers with flair.
Worms wear spectacles to read the news,
While frogs in tuxedos sing the blues.

The trees hold hands and sway in glee,
As butterflies gossip, oh what a spree!
The grass tickles toes of passing shoes,
In a world where the silly can't refuse.

Clouds play hide and seek with the sun,
As raindrops giggle, oh what fun!
Nature conducts a zany troupe,
In this circus where all creatures loop.

Let's frolic in this whimsical plot,
With laughter that's shared and joy that's caught.
Where every heart beats in lighthearted tune,
And the stars giggle softly, under the moon.

Fables Beneath the Twilight

At dusk, the critters don their hats,
A squirrel strums tunes amidst the chats,
Rabbits dance, their tails a-flap,
While fireflies jump in a glowing clap.

Frogs croak tales of olden times,
As owls hoot out their riddled rhymes,
A hedgehog leads a conga line,
With all the woodland beings feeling fine.

The moon peeks out, oh what a sight,
With laughter ringing through the night,
A bear shares stories, oh so grand,
While ants march round with snacks in hand.

At dawn, the fun begins to fade,
But memories linger from the parade,
With smiles shared in twilight's glow,
The joy of the woods forever flows.

Rhymes of the Ancient Oak

Beneath the branches, whispers play,
A lazy cat naps all day,
While squirrels debate the best snack,
A gathering of friends, never lack.

The wise old owl, with glasses round,
Tells jokes that echo through the sound,
A burly raccoon adds his flair,
With antics that leave all in despair.

A dance-off breaks out near the roots,
With mushrooms sprouting hip-hop boots,
The wind tunes in, adding notes,
As even the shyest creature gloats.

As shadows stretch, the fun winds down,
But stories linger in the crown,
And laughter bounces in the air,
For every tree knows how to care.

Myths Woven in Midnight

Under starlight, tales take flight,
A bear plays poker, what a sight!
Foxes cheer, a raucous crowd,
While owls hoot their cheers out loud.

A hedgehog spins a yarn so tall,
About a fish who danced at the ball,
Crickets chirp their rhythmic tune,
At this wild party, oh so strewn!

The moonlight glimmers on a game,
As everyone shouts, "Who's to blame?"
The trees lean in to catch each jest,
While laughter bubbles, it's the best.

At dawn's arrival, the fun must cease,
Yet stories echo, bringing peace,
In dreams, they'll twirl and leap again,
For joy in night's lull never ends.

Serenades of a Forgotten Path

Along the trail, where shadows creep,
A goat sings ballads, oh so deep,
With sheep in tow, they frolic about,
Turning every frown inside-out.

The breeze joins in with a gentle hum,
As raccoons beat drums, making a thrum,
A flower dances, all bright and bold,
In this whimsical world, stories unfold.

The path twists on with giggles and glee,
With each step taken, more fun to see,
A fox recites a haiku or two,
While turtles race, oh how they flew!

As twilight dances, the fun moves near,
And woodland creatures draw close to hear,
Each serenade and witty quip,
In the heart of the woods, friendships grip.

Legends of the Leafy Labyrinth

In a maze of greens, so tightly spun,
The squirrels debate who's got the most fun.
A rabbit in sunglasses, so cool, so sly,
Dancing with shadows, as owls just sigh.

Between twisted roots, the gossip takes flight,
A hedgehog claims he can stargaze at night.
Tales of lost acorns, and crowns made of leaves,
Every tall tale makes the woodland believe.

With each rustling branch, laughter prevails,
In the whimsical woods where nonsense never fails.
Myth of a squirrel who flew on a kite,
Leaves spinning tales in the glow of twilight.

In leafy theatres, they put on a show,
Of acorn-wearing mice that steal the show.
The magic of mirth flows through every vine,
In this leafy labyrinth, all jokes align.

Melodies of the Mindful Mist

In the misty morn, where giggles reside,
A fox with a flute takes fashion in stride.
The fog sings a tune that tickles the air,
While frogs in their hats perform without care.

Dewdrops are drummers, so rhythmic and bright,
Bouncing on petals, they bring pure delight.
A melody plays from an owl's little wing,
As crickets join in with a zing and a zing.

The chirp of a bird is a comedic burst,
Mixing up notes, oh, how it is cursed!
While turtles try to keep up on their feet,
Unruly musicians, who never play neat.

In the hazy embrace, where laughter takes flight,
Every creature finds joy in the soft twilight.
The tunes weave together like threads of a quilt,
In this misty wonder, all worries are spilt.

Lyrical Reveries of the Radiant

Beneath the bright sun, where shadows retreat,
A parrot on stilts shows off his own beat.
He juggles ripe fruit with a wink of an eye,
While llamas in hats pass leisurely by.

Daisies debate the best dance of the day,
With butterflies laughing and joining the fray.
A sunflower shrugs, "I can out-twist you all!"
While daisies just giggle and start to fall.

In radiant realms, where nonsense runs free,
A crab plays the piano, so silly, so glee.
His claws tap away in a curious way,
Turning the garden into cabaret.

So join in the fun, as the sun spins around,
In a whirl of bright colors, joy knows no bound.
With rhymes floating high like balloons in the air,
These lyrical tales are beyond all compare.

Tides of Ancient Tapestry

In the depths of the sea, where the giggles abound,
A turtle named Timmy swims round and round.
In a cloak woven tight from kelp and old fame,
He tells tales of jellyfish, all underwater fame.

The octopus spins yarns with eight arms in play,
While seahorses giggle and dance in ballet.
Seashells gossip, oh what a delight,
Of crabs who wear crowns and sing songs of the night.

The currents carry whispers of fish dressed so fine,
Buffalo of bubbles that swirl and entwine.
From brine-soaked adventures to shenanigans bold,
In this vibrant tapestry, the stories unfold.

With tides that pulse lively, and waves with a grin,
The ocean's great tales beckon all who swim in.
So dive into laughter, let currents set free,
In the watery depths, where we all want to be.

Artistry in the Woodland Palette

In the forest, squirrels paint,
With acorns as their tool,
A masterpiece of nuts and leaves,
Who knew they'd break the rule?

Mushrooms wear a polka dot,
Dressed up for a ball tonight,
Bouncing bugs in disco mode,
Glimpse this wild delight!

A raccoon plays a tune so sweet,
On drums of hollow wood,
The trees all sway to his beat,
In this neighborhood!

Nature's jesters bumbling forth,
With laughter in the breeze,
Artistry of furry pals,
Creating fun with ease!

Tapestry of Forgotten Ferns

In the shade, the ferns conspire,
To weave a coat for bees,
They giggle at the sunlight,
Now that's a funny tease!

A snail slips on a fern, oh no!
It spins a dizzy dance,
With every wiggle, laughter grows,
Who knew it had a chance?

The toadstools form a circus scene,
With acrobats so bold,
Jumping high above the ground,
Their antics never old!

Forgotten ferns still dream of fun,
In shadows where they play,
With whispers shared of mischief,
They bloom in their own way!

Whispers of Timeless Tales

A jester bug spins yarns of gold,
To insects gathered near,
He spins tales of the midnight owls,
And how they won the beer!

Grasshoppers exchange their vows,
To dance beneath the moon,
Their froggy friends just hop along,
And join the merry tune!

Squirrels write in ancient trees,
Of brave deeds long ago,
But mostly tales of snack attacks,
That always steal the show!

Beneath the stars, the stories flow,
With giggles in the night,
Timeless whispers fill the air,
In nature's pure delight!

Echoes of Enchanted Pages

An owl reads riddles upside down,
A mystery quite absurd,
With whispers echoing through the night,
The forest not disturbed!

A clever fox, with wit so sly,
Claims he's the author too,
He pens his life in quirky rhymes,
With side notes that amuse!

The dandelions play tag with wind,
Their seeds take flight like dreams,
Racing past the laughing brook,
In whimsical moonbeams!

Echoes of a bedtime story,
Alive beneath the trees,
In pages filled with laughter,
Where nature finds her ease!

Ballads of the Verdant Veil

In the green of the wood, where the squirrels sing,
Frogs wear crowns made of leaves, it's a silly thing.
A rabbit in slippers dances on its toes,
While the shy hedgehogs debate wearing bows.

The trees chuckle low at the antics below,
As the owl plays chess with a chipmunk named Joe.
Raccoons throw parties with snacks for the night,
And the moonlight just giggles, oh what a sight!

With fireflies buzzing, a jazz band of light,
They twirl and they twist, oh what a delight!
The badgers declare, "Let's all wear a hat!"
While the wise old tortoise shouts, "Not like that!"

Each night in the veil, a new caper unfolds,
With laughter and joy, each story retold.
In the heart of the woods, where the fun never fails,
Sing loud, all ye creatures, in playful details!

Secrets Entwined in Roots

Underneath the surface, where secrets reside,
The worms tell jokes while the moles take a ride.
A beetle in glasses reads books in the dark,
While a snail in a cap plays a lyrical lark.

In hidden caverns where shadows reside,
Batty bats laugh as they take an odd glide.
A gopher spins tales of the cheese he once stole,
While the newts in the pond just laugh from their shoal.

Twisted vines giggle, entwined in their grip,
As the roots tell their stories, sharing each quip.
A fox with a wink brings a tale out of time,
While the fireflies flicker, adding rhythm and rhyme.

In the whispering earth, where the antics are grand,
Creatures unite, as they all understand.
With secrets and laughter that help them to thrive,
In the roots of the world, all the fun comes alive!

Phantoms of the Woodland Whisper

In the twilight's embrace, where the shadows dance free,
A ghost in a tutu twirls under the tree.
The owls hoot in laughter, with jokes overhead,
While the spirits tell tales of the pranks that they've led.

The breezes bring whispers of mischief untold,
With fairies in frolic and goblins so bold.
A wisp with a giggle floats high in the air,
Sharing secrets and puns with the mushrooms down there.

As the moonlight peeks in, it tickles the leaves,
While the phantoms all chuckle, wearing their sleeves.
Each rustle and rustle brings stories anew,
Of a ghost who once lost a bet to a shoe!

In the woodland's embrace, where unity shines,
The echo of laughter through shadowed designs.
With phantoms and giggles in a whimsical spree,
Nature's fun-loving spirit is wild and carefree!

Tales from the Echoing Pines

Beneath lofty branches where echoes delight,
A pinecone debates if it's left or it's right.
The squirrels play opera, a nutty charade,
While the chipmunks hold court, all laughs on parade.

The trees start to sway, with rhythm and rhyme,
As the wind whispers secrets, all in good time.
A bear croons a ballad, his voice deep and low,
While the mice tap their feet, helping the show.

In the heart of the pines, tales sparkle with cheer,
From a fox who once wandered, now thinks he's a deer.
A raccoon in sneakers steals cookies at night,
And the owls hoot, "Encore!" till the morning light.

With laughter resounding through forest so bright,
In tales of the pines, mirth takes glorious flight.
So gather, dear friends, in this woodland of glee,
The echoing stories bring fun and esprit!

Sonnet of the Elysian Fields

In fields of green where daisies dance,
A cow with shades gives all a glance.
She winks and grins, a funny sight,
While munching grass from morn to night.

The sheep, they laugh, in woolly glee,
As goats perform a grand marquee.
They prance about, a silly show,
The kind that makes your belly grow.

A squirrel jams with acorn tunes,
While ducks are tap dancing with moons.
Oh, laughter swells, in skies so blue,
In these bright fields where joy breaks through.

So let's rejoice, both large and small,
For laughter's fun is meant for all.
In fields where happiness grows wide,
We'll share our giggles side by side.

Stanzas of Sorrowed Shadows

In shadows cast, a cat did creep,
While dreaming of a fish to leap.
But tripped on strings of yarn galore,
And tumbled hard, then sought the door.

The mice convene, they plot and scheme,
To chase away the feline dream.
Their tiny feet go pitter-pat,
As they conspire 'gainst that silly cat.

A ghost appears and starts to moan,
But sneezes loud, this spirit's known.
With every scare, it sends a shiver,
Yet all it gains is laughs and slivers.

So shadows hover, but do not stay,
For laughter turns their gloom to play.
In every corner where they dwell,
A giggle rises, casting spells.

Timeless Winds of Wisdom

Oh wise old trees with branches wide,
They whisper tales of joy and pride.
One said, "Turn that frown upside down,
A pair of squirrels just stole my crown!"

With gentle winds that swirl and swirl,
They tell of wisdom—dizzy twirl.
A leaf drops down, and lands on heads,
And giggles burst from crazy spreads.

A turtle slow, with dreams in tow,
Advises all to take it slow.
But frogs proclaim, "Let's leap and bound!
Quick-hopping's where true fun is found!"

So gather 'round, both slow and fast,
In nature's jokes, our laughs will last.
For wisdom's found in every breeze,
In every chuckle, joy's the key.

Songs of the Celestial Canopy

Beneath the stars, a raccoon sings,
A tune of mischief and shiny things.
It juggles moons and comets bright,
Tickling clouds with sheer delight.

The owls debate, with sage-like grace,
Who stole the moon? A furry face?
They hoot and holler, "Not my style,
I've been here nesting all the while!"

While constellations twinkle in jest,
A comet zooms, it's quite the guest.
It zips around, and we all cheer,
With every loop, it brings us near.

So join the dance, where comedy reigns,
In cosmic laughter, joy remains.
In skies adorned with sparkly hues,
The universe hums its rollicking tunes.

Chronicles in Moonlight

A cat in a hat danced under the stars,
Chasing fireflies, dodging passing cars.
With each little leap, a giggle would burst,
As an owl hooted loud, oh how he was cursed!

The raccoons gathered, a band of three,
Playing old tunes on a broken TV.
They strummed on a broom and drummed with a spoon,
While squirrels joined in with their acorn tune!

The moon winked down, a mischievous sight,
As the night wore on, full of joy and delight.
A frog croaked a beat, tapping feet all around,
In this comical tale, laughter abound!

When dawn started rising, the fun was all gone,
But the memories lingered, their spirits shone on.
They promised to meet for another moon's glow,
In the land of the funny, where friendship can flow.

Starlit Stories Untold

Under the stars, with a wink and a smile,
A penguin slipped on ice, fell down with style.
His friends rolled with laughter, oh what a sight,
As he flopped like a seal in the cool of the night!

A hedgehog in glasses read tales of romance,
Though every plot twist caused him to prance.
He stumbled on words, misheard all the lines,
Making stories of love meet the fizz of the times!

A rabbit with jokes took the stage with flair,
Telling puns to the crowd, his humor laid bare.
With hop after hop, he spun tales so grand,
Leaving giggles and snorts, all perfectly planned!

So gather 'round friends for this whimsical show,
Under the bright stars, let your laughter flow.
In this shining moment, let worries take flight,
For stories are funny in the warmth of the night!

Songs from the Forest's Heart

Deep in the woods, where the wildflowers cheer,
An awkward deer danced, bringing everyone near.
He tripped on a root, fell flat on his face,
And the birds burst with laughter all over the place!

A raccoon recited his best stand-up bits,
While the badgers all chuckled, each rolling in fits.
With a wink and a joke, he stole every scene,
Making friends laugh hard, you know what I mean!

The trees joined the fun, swayed to the beat,
With branches that waved like they were on their feet.
A breeze did a spin, whispering a jest,
In this forest of giggles, life truly is best!

So here in the woods, where laughter cascades,
Every critter is merry, their joy never fades.
Embrace the delight, let your worries depart,
With the songs from the forest that live in each heart!

Verses of the Wandering Willow

A willow tree pondered, swaying side to side,
Dreaming of travels, with a comical stride.
Her branches reached out, giving hugs to the breeze,
While grinning at squirrels scurrying with ease!

A fox with a backpack came whistling through,
With a map made of crumbs; oh what a view!
He got lost in his thoughts, missed the path he should take,
Singing silly songs about a big chocolate cake!

The willow just chuckled, her leaves danced and twirled,
While the moon played peek-a-boo, lighting the world.
With each gentle sway, she shared tales so grand,
Of laughter and friendship that flourished at hand!

So celebrate life, in all its odd ways,
With verses that make you laugh for days.
For in every giggle, and each silly jest,
Lies the beauty of living, and this is the best!

Journeys Through the Whispering Understory

In a meadow bright, I lost my shoe,
A rabbit laughed, what more could I do?
We danced in circles, unplanned ballet,
A squirrel critiqued in a furiously gray.

With acorns as hats, we formed a parade,
Inviting the bugs, in the sun, we played.
A worm stole the show with his breakdance twist,
While birds in the sky sang, "You simply can't miss!"

A mushroom stood tall, claiming kingly reign,
But fell with a thud, oh what a disdain!
We rolled on the ground, laughter untamed,
Hailing the shroom, forever unnamed.

Back home at dusk, with tales spun bright,
Of shoes that go missing and rabbits in flight.
The woods whispered secrets, both funny and true,
Next time I'll bring snacks, and a shoe or two!

Sonatas of the Celestial Glade

Under the stars where the crickets play,
A tree said, "Hey! Let's dance the night away!"
I stepped on a twig, it squeaked like a tire,
And the moonlit breeze filled the glade with a choir.

With shadows for partners, we bumped and we swayed,
While owls in the branches formed their own brigade.
They hooted and hollered as we spun in delight,
Until someone tripped, oh, the hilarious sight!

A deer in the corner tried to moonwalk too,
But slipped on a patch of the morning dew.
With giggles and snickers, we cheered it along,
While the stars in the heavens joined in with a song.

When dawn finally came, our dance came to end,
But the memories lingered, this night was a blend.
Of laughter and joy in that mystical glade,
Where trees and the critters our antics paraded.

Riddles Beneath the Ancient Foliage

Beneath the great trees where shadows conspire,
A riddle was posed by an old, wise briar.
"What runs but can't walk, and twirls like the breeze?"
I scratched my head, while bees buzzed with glee.

A cheeky young fox then chimed in with a song,
"It's water, my friend! Now don't get me wrong!"
But the raven nearby just cawed with a grin,
"Y'all need to watch where the laughter begins!"

We gathered our clues like tasty ripe fruit,
Each answer we whispered made the others hoot.
A squirrel tossed out nuts, calling them clues,
As leaves started giggling with every excuse.

As twilight approached, our riddles fell flat,
"What do you call a tree that loves to chat?"
We argued and laughed, till the moonlight shone bright,
And the foliage echoed with joy through the night.

Chants of the Nightshade Borders

At the edge of the woods, where shadows collide,
The frogs held a meeting with crickets beside.
"What's green and can jump but won't win a race?"
They laughed at their answers, each one was a face!

A toad croaked a tune, a grand serenade,
While fireflies danced with their glow on parade.
With each wily whisper and quirky refrain,
They joked 'bout the moon, who looked just like grain!

The hedgehogs rolled in, their spines in a fuss,
Declaring, "This party is quite ridiculous!"
A dance-off commenced, with twirls and with spins,
As shadows grew longer and laughter broke in.

With a chant of delight, we serenaded the night,
Underneath the twinkle of stars burning bright.
In the borders where nightshade brought fun without end,
We basked in the joy of a whimsical blend.

Sonnets of Serene Shadows

In shadows where the giggles sprout,
A squirrel wears a tiny pout.
He lost his acorn in a dance,
Now prancing 'round, he takes a chance.

The moonlight winks upon his tail,
While hedgehogs start their nightly tale.
A rabbit hops in silly shoes,
And gives a speech to dainty hues.

Atop a tree, a wise old crow,
Tells jokes that only squirrels know.
With feathered friends, he laughs away,
As night unfolds its bright ballet.

To all who wander through the wood,
Join in the jests, it's all quite good!
Beneath the stars, the laughs will flow,
As woodland critters steal the show.

Stanzas of the Silken Stream

By the stream where ripples sing,
A frog croaks out a funny fling.
With flies on stilts, he leaps and glides,
While fish take bets in their fishy hides.

The turtles wear their spectacles high,
Debating on who can make the best pie.
They read the recipe from a leaf,
But ended up in a pastry grief!

An otter and a beaver fight,
Who can build the wobbliest kite.
With twigs and twine, they spin and weave,
Then watch their craft begin to leave.

"Oh, hold it back!" the otter cries,
While the beaver laughs and rudely spies.
Through chuckles wide, the waters gleam,
As ripples dance in silly dream.

Chronicles in the Quiet Glade

In quiet glades where wild things roam,
A deer in pajamas feels right at home.
With curls so big and antics grand,
She prances 'round, no care at hand.

A hedgehog in a hat so fine,
Pretends to sip a mug of wine.
With friends nearby, they all agree,
To hold a ball beneath the tree.

The grass provides a dancing floor,
As crickets chirp and squirrels roar.
They twirl and swirl in nature's light,
In leaps of joy, they end the night.

With laughter ringing through the glade,
They share the stories never made.
A night so wild, a memory bold,
With every giggle, magic's told.

Harmonies of Heartfelt Happenings

Within the grove, a laugh parade,
With dancing ants, a grand charade.
A ladybug sings a catchy tune,
While crickets swing under the moon.

A bear who's juggling berries bright,
Drops them all, what a funny sight!
With every bounce, the laughter grows,
As friends roll 'round in berry clothes.

Next to the bush, a wise old owl,
Shares jokes that make the foxes howl.
With puns and quips that ken the night,
Their giggle-fest is sheer delight.

So gather 'round, all creatures keen,
Let friendship bloom in shades of green.
Through trials, laughs, and heartfelt cheer,
A tapestry of joy appears.

Fables Woven in Bark

In the forest, trees tell tales,
Of squirrels in tiny scales.
They dance with glee, chase a breeze,
While rabbits giggle in the leaves.

Once a crow wore a shiny hat,
Started a trend, imagine that!
The owl hooted, quite bemused,
Chasing squirrels, never refused.

The hedgehog dreamed of flighty things,
With bigger dreams than sprouting wings.
But when he tried, oh what a sight,
He rolled away in pure delight!

A wise old tree holds laughter tight,
As whispers weave through day and night.
Each branch a story, twist and twirled,
In this funny, leafy world.

Symphonies of the Ancient Grove

In the grove, the band plays loud,
Dancing bumbles, gather 'round!
Beetles thump on logs so stout,
While chipmunks join the lively rout.

A raccoon sings with flair and pride,
But forgets his pants, oh what a ride!
His friends can't help but point and laugh,
As he shimmies with a wobbly half.

A songbird glides with fancy notes,
While frogs in chorus croak from moats.
Even crickets join in the spree,
Turning the night into a melody!

In this grove, joy never hides,
It's where the silly heart abides.
With every beat, a shout, a cheer,
Symphonies of laughter fill the sphere.

Legends Carved in Shadows

In shadows deep, a tale unfolds,
Of a caterpillar brave and bold.
He thought he'd twist into a knight,
But ended up a silly sight!

The squirrel claimed to know it all,
But tripped and made a clumsy fall.
His acorn hat flew through the air,
And landed squarely on a bear!

A woodland fox with tricks galore,
Tried to juggle nuts, but dropped four.
They rolled away and down a hill,
Chasing after them, what a thrill!

So gather 'round, young and old,
For shadows dance with stories told.
Each laugh a spark, each giggle bright,
Legends woven in delight.

Melodies of the Moonlit Thicket

In the thicket, moonlight shines,
Where shadows twist like silly lines.
A fox breaks out in funky dance,
With owls hooting, lost in trance.

The fireflies blink a bright encore,
While all the critters beg for more.
A turtle tried to take the lead,
But took a nap instead, well indeed!

Dancing twigs and rustling leaves,
Make joyful tunes that never cleave.
Each creature sways to nature's beat,
As laughter rustles through the street.

Oh moonlit nights, with fun galore,
A secret jam behind each door.
In this thicket, life's a tune,
We'll dance beneath the cheerful moon.

Rhythms of the Rushing River

In a river that laughed and splashed,
A fish wore a hat made of trash.
He danced with the breeze, all in good cheer,
Saying, "Come join me for a drink, my dear!"

The ducks held a concert, quacking their tunes,
While frogs hopped about like jazzy baboons.
A turtle slid by, with a wink and a shout,
"Don't be so slow, come and check it out!"

Rocks tumbled down with a giggle so bright,
They whispered of secrets all through the night.
The river chuckled, a playful delight,
As it tickled the banks in a water-wrapped fight.

So if you're down by that bubbly old stream,
Don't forget your laughter, let it beam.
For in every ripple, a joke's to be found,
In the rhythms of water, joy does abound.

Lore of the Luminous Leaves

Once in a tree that wore colors so bold,
A squirrel found acorns that glittered like gold.
He threw them around, sharing joy with a wink,
"Let's make a salad! Just don't let it stink!"

Leaves rustled softly, gossiping high,
About the strange bird who just learned to fly.
He flapped and he floundered, a sight quite absurd,
And sang to the world, though no one had heard.

The mushrooms below held a dance in the dark,
Inviting the critters, each one a spark.
With twirls and with leaps, all the fun they conjured,
Made even the owls stop hooting and ponder.

In this realm of enchantment, laughter takes root,
Wraps round every branch, a whimsical suit.
So stop by this forest, where joy lifts the eaves,
And dance with the laughter in luminous leaves.

Echoes of Ethereal Existence

In a realm where the shadows all giggled in tones,
A ghost told a joke to a pile of stones.
They chuckled a bit, then rolled off with glee,
As the moonlight danced on a magical spree.

Fairies were buzzing with laughter so bright,
Combing their hair with beams of moonlight.
A sprite brought marshmallows to roast in the air,
Claiming, "This campfire is beyond compare!"

The clouds were all bursting with silly chortles,
While stars spun around in their sparkly whirl.
"Life's too short!" they announced with a flare,
"Let's tickle the nighttime with frolic and dare!"

In a world where the echoes just giggle and sway,
Thank the comical cosmos for a whimsical play.
For every sweet whisper, a story unspun,
In the echoes of existence, we all find our fun.

Fables from Forgotten Forests

In a woodland so quirky, with tales yet untold,
A rabbit wore glasses, looking quite bold.
He read from a book on carrot cuisine,
And all of the creatures queued up for a scene.

A wise old owl spoke in riddles and rhymes,
About the odd habits of squirrels at night times.
"Nuts in pajamas and acorns galore,
They tap dance on stumps, then beg for much more!"

Beneath ancient trees, where the shadows did play,
The raccoons threw parties at the end of the day.
With cookies made of berries, they danced like mad fools,

Proclaiming, "We're royalty! Let's break all the rules!"

So wander these woods where the laughter runs free,
And find all the fables that welcome with glee.
For in forgotten forests, the joy does not end,
Where whimsy and wonder become the best blend.

Harmonies of the Hidden Glade

Beneath the trees where squirrels play,
A frog has stolen my croaking sway.
I caught him dancing on a log,
Wearing a crown made of misty fog.

The owls hoot tunes like jazz at night,
While fireflies flicker, providing light.
Bunnies tap dance, oh what a sight,
Wiggling their noses with all their might.

Mice are moonwalkers, they scurry and glide,
Avoiding the cat who's lost his pride.
With every giggle, the forest sways,
A comedy club in nature's rays.

So come, my friend, to this merry place,
Where laughter echoes in leafy space.
Let's join the critters in raucous cheer,
In the glade where fun is always near.

Scribbles on the Whispering Wind

A gust of breeze, it tickles my ear,
Whispers of secrets, oh so near.
The trees gossip about my bad puns,
As grasshoppers laugh and play with the sun.

Doodles of clouds drift lazily by,
Making funny faces, oh me, oh my!
One rain drop plops on my nose with a tease,
While tulips yawn and stretch with ease.

A rabbit rolls over, falling in style,
While butterflies flutter, wearing a smile.
I scribble my dreams on the blades of green,
In the humor of nature, I feel like a queen.

So chase the breeze and giggle along,
Let whimsy be heard in life's silly song.
With each gentle breeze, joy gets unspooled,
In the dance of the wind, we are all fools.

Rhythms of the Twilight Arbor

Under the arch of branches so wide,
A sloth in a sunhat, what a wild ride!
He's groovin' slowly, with style and flair,
While squirrels bust moves without a care.

The shadows stretch long, the day feels cheeky,
A raccoon's stealing snacks, oh so sneaky!
With each clumsy step, he trips on a root,
Landing face-first in a pile of fruit.

A band of crickets plays tunes soft and low,
While fireflies twinkle, putting on a show.
With every beat, the twilight sings,
Of laughter, mischief, and wobbly wings.

So join the party, bring your best cheer,
In this twilight grove, there's nothing to fear.
With laughter and rhythms, the night takes flight,
Under the arbor where joy shines bright.

Memoirs Beneath the Canopy

Deep in the woods, where secrets unfold,
A turtle tells tales, both funny and old.
With every slow blink, wisdom he shares,
About the time he outran a pair of bears!

The leaves rustle softly, a giggle or two,
As beetles debate who's the best in the crew.
A snail on a mission, planner of dreams,
Writes down his goals with quills and streams.

Beneath the bright canopy, night has a grin,
While hedgehogs toast marshmallows, it's a win!
With laughter and stories, our hearts take wing,
In memoirs of fun, we find joy in spring.

So pull up a chair, come join this delight,
Where every creature shines in the night.
Beneath this green cover, the funny times soar,
In memories we craft, let's laugh evermore.

Reflections at Dusk

At dusk the frogs hold court, quite loud,
They croak like they're the wisest crowd.
A cricket joins with a violin tune,
While rabbits grab snacks and dance under the moon.

The fireflies blink in a silly chase,
Bumping into one another, what a race!
A hedgehog laughs, but pricks his own back,
Squeaks of joy, then away he'll pack.

A wise owl hoots with a wink in his eye,
"Life's a riot, now watch me fly!"
In the midst of laughter and nature's delight,
Even the stars giggle, shining so bright.

So here's to the creatures that light up the night,
In their quirky ballet, oh what a sight!
With a croak and a chirp, we all heed the call,
Join the fun, come one, come all!

Narratives in the Leaves

The leaves tell tales with a rustle and sway,
Of the squirrels who party at the break of day.
They spin silly stories, each twist a delight,
As chipmunks break out in a wobbly fight.

The big oak tree chuckles, 'Oh what a scene,'
As branches hang low, dressed in bright green.
A breeze whispers secrets, a giggle on cue,
"Did you hear what the crow did? Oh, wait till you do!"

With acorns as treasures and twigs as their ploys,
The woodland critters make plenty of noise.
In every crisp leaf, a laugh that remains,
A string of sweet jokes woven in veins.

So gather the stories, oh what a treat,
In the forest's embrace, there's joy to repeat.
With every soft flutter, and rustle anew,
Nature reveals a comedy just for you.

Chronicles of the Gentle Breeze

The breeze comes whistling with a playful grin,
Whirling through flowers, let the fun begin!
It tickles the daisies, gives roses a spin,
While joking with sunbeams, it sweeps right in.

"Hey there, old tree, don't be so stiff,
Dance with the petals, give the world a lift!"
But the tree just waves, its branches so grand,
"Dear breeze, I've got roots, I can't make a stand."

Through meadows it traipses, instigating cheer,
Making butterflies giggle, collecting their sneers.
With whispers of laughter, each whisper a jest,
The world turns a chuckle, a jovial quest.

So whenever you feel a cool breeze on your face,
Remember its riddles, its playful embrace.
For in nature's grand book, each page is a tease,
A chronicle penned by the gentle breeze.

Poetry of the Silent Stream

The stream flows softly, a bubbly delight,
It trips over rocks, with giggles and light.
Each splash is a verse, each ripple a rhyme,
As pebbles chuckle, lost in their time.

Fish dart like ink, writing stories below,
The water sings softly, with a humorous flow.
"Watch out!" says a turtle, slow as can be,
But the fish simply wink, "We're fast, you'll see!"

A log stretches out, tired from the day,
Sharing his dreams in a quirky ballet.
Birds perch nearby, tuning in to the glee,
As each line of water gleefully agrees.

So next time you wander by streams with a gleam,
Listen well to their laughter, their whimsical dream.
In each little bubble, a sonnet, a cheer,
In the flow of life, there's joy everywhere near.

Tales of the Wistful Woodland

In the forest, a squirrel debates,
Whether to dance or to drop down crates.
Leaves giggle as they flutter around,
While a rabbit jumps high, making quite a sound.

A wise old owl in glasses so round,
Tells jokes to the trees, they laugh, then rebound.
A raccoon plays piano with paws made for snacks,
While chipmunks tap dance, wearing small hats.

The mushrooms are stoic, quite settled in place,
But a wandering fungus starts a wild race.
A hedgehog in rollerskates zooms by in a flash,
Leaving laughter and chaos, a hilariously bash.

In the glen, the creatures share puns and glee,
As the sun dips low, it's a sight to see.
A tea party starts with peculiar toppings,
No one can stop and the laughter keeps popping.

Songs of the Singing Stones

The stones sing sweetly, or so they claim,
With voices so gravelly, they sound quite lame.
A pebble named Pete leads the off-key choir,
While boulders giggle, tossed in the fire.

One rock tells tales of a time long ago,
When it rolled down a hill, feeling quite the show.
It tripped on a root, flew up in a spin,
Landed in mud and said, 'Wasn't that a win?'

With a beat of their chests, they stomp and they stamp,
A rhythm so quirky, it's more like a cramp.
A shiny old marble thinks it's quite grand,
Slick with its polish, it takes center stand.

But the older the stones, the worse the joke are,
One said, 'Why do rocks never use cars?'
'Because they don't want to be gravel-ed away,
They prefer to just sit and bask in the day!'

Whimsy of the Willow's Whisper

The willow tree whispers with a giggle so light,
Telling secrets to squirrels who scamper at night.
Its branches are draped like a very bad dress,
But it feels like a queen in its leafy finesse.

A frog on a lily pad croaks a loud rhyme,
Trying to catch bugs while keeping in time.
'Why did the fish refuse to eat cake?'
'It didn't want a bad case of bellyache!'

The wind plays tag, while the leaves do a jig,
A mouse in a tuxedo performs a small fig.
With acorns like maracas, there's music in air,
Every critter and creature sings, without a care.

As twilight spills laughter, the moon starts to beam,
Lighting the antics of this whimsical dream.
With twirls and with sways, in this wood so bizarre,
The willow just chuckles, a true superstar.

Prose of the Pensive Pines

Tall pines ponder life like philosophers grand,
While needles drop down like applause from a band.
One pine says, 'Why are we tall and so wise?
Maybe it's all just a funny disguise!'

The forest floor giggles at their lofty thoughts,
As a hedgehog in spectacles scribbles in knots.
'If trees could wear shoes, would they trip on their roots?'
A toddler's laughter echoes, their humor like hoots.

A woodpecker nearby pecks at a plan,
To build the best nest with a can-do elan.
While ants hold a parade to show off their gear,
Spreading joy in the forest, giving a cheer.

At dusk, when the shadows stretch long from the trees,
The pines share their tales in the soft evening breeze.
With each whispered story, a chuckle so bright,
Proving wisdom can come wrapped up in delight.

www.ingramcontent.com/pod-product-compliance
Lightning Source LLC
Chambersburg PA
CBHW071837160426
43209CB00003B/329